STUFF THAT SUCKS

a teen's guide to accepting what you can't change *and* committing to what you can

BEN SEDLEY

Instant Help Books
An Imprint of New Harbinger Publications, Inc.

"Put simply, *Stuff That Sucks* is good stuff! Short and to the point, it can help teens from thirteen to at least forty-nine learn to handle life's yucky stuff in a way that will help them get to the good stuff. Far from being a stuffy psych book, this is a concise how-to guide to the stuff that really counts: living a life free from getting stuffed by the stuff that sucks."

> —Benjamin Schoendorff, MA, MSc, founder of the Contextual Psychology Institute in Montreal, QC, Canada; international acceptance and commitment therapy (ACT) trainer; and coauthor of the recent *The Essential Guide to the ACT Matrix* and *The ACT Practitioner's Guide to the Science of Compassion*

"I love *Stuff That Sucks*! It is a pithy, genuine, and skillful application of ACT for adolescents. As a compassion-focused therapy (CFT) practitioner, I think this book is a wonderful way to help adolescents meet the stuff that sucks in their lives with acceptance, self-compassion, and the courageous willingness to get their lives moving toward the things that matter to them. I can guarantee that I'll be using it with my own clients. Highly recommended!"

> —Russell Kolts, PhD, professor of psychology at Eastern Washington University, and author of *CFT Made Simple* and *The Compassionate-Mind Guide to Managing Your Anger*

"Undoubtedly, sometimes life sucks. It can be difficult, painful, and filled with big scary things. And within this realization, opens up a whole new way to approach these experiences—one without constant fighting and struggling with thoughts and feelings that are often out of our control. In this book, Ben brings together the cutting-edge ideas from psychology to help you mindfully choose the life you want. It's written in a simple and fun way to make it useful for young people and parents alike. Written with wisdom and wit, this outstanding book is set to become a self-help classic."

> —Joe Oliver, PhD, director at Contextual Consulting, and coauthor of *ACTivate Your Life*

"In *Stuff That Sucks*, Ben Sedley takes the key elements of ACT, and presents them in ways that are immediately accessible, relatable, and actionable. Indeed, I would rate it as a must-have for every adolescent's bookshelf."

> —Tiffany Rochester, clinical psychologist at The Charles Street Clinic in North Perth, Australia

"I love this book! It's a great gift for parents to give their teenage kids, and a fantastic resource for therapists working with adolescents. Ben admirably pulls off the hat trick of making ACT simple, practical, and very entertaining. *Stuff That Sucks* is really stuff that rocks!"

—**Russ Harris**, author of *The Happiness Trap* and *ACT Made Simple*

"Fast-paced, fun, and useful, this book shows how to deal with stuff that sucks. It's all scientifically based, but you'll be having too much fun to notice. This book absolutely, positively, does not suck."

—**Steven C. Hayes, PhD**, codeveloper of ACT, and author of *Get Out of Your Mind and Into Your Life*

"Ben Sedley has written a wonderful book for teens. A must-have for the collection.
Stuff That Sucks delivers with powerful images, clear messages on what it means to be a human, and lots of ideas for helping teens. A fabulous book."

—**Louise Hayes, PhD**, coauthor of *The Thriving Adolescent* and *Get Out of Your Mind and Into Your Life for Teens*

STUFF THAT SUCKS

Publisher's Note

First published in Great Britain in 2015 by Robinson.

Distributed in Canada by Raincoast Books

Copyright © 2017 by Ben Sedley
    Instant Help Books
    An imprint of New Harbinger Publications, Inc.
    5674 Shattuck Avenue
    Oakland, CA 94609
    www.newharbinger.com

Cover design by Amy Shoup

Original book design by Open Lab, Massey University (Catherine Adam, Kalos Chan, and Chloe Johnston)

Library of Congress Cataloging-in-Publication Data

Names: Sedley, Ben, author.

Title: Stuff that sucks : a teen's guide to accepting what you can't change and committing to what you can / Ben Sedley.

Description: Oakland, CA : Instant Help, 2017. | Series: The instant help solutions series | Audience: Age: 14-18.

Identifiers: LCCN 2016028112 (print) | LCCN 2016048175 (ebook) | ISBN 9781626258655 (paperback) | ISBN 9781626258662 (pdf e-book) | ISBN 9781626258679 (epub) | ISBN 9781626258662 (PDF e-book) | ISBN 9781626258679 (ePub)

Subjects: LCSH: Affect (Psychology)--Juvenile literature. | Emotions in adolescence--Juvenile literature. | Adolescent psychology--Juvenile literature.

Classification: LCC BF175.5.A35 S33 2017 (print) | LCC BF175.5.A35 (ebook) | DDC 155.5/19--dc23

LC record available at https://lccn.loc.gov/2016028112

19   18   17

10   9   8   7   6   5   4   3   2   1   First Printing

STUFF ABOUT THIS BOOK

Don't believe a word I say.

I'm not claiming to have all the answers for everyone.

I don't know you, so who am I to tell you what will make things better for you?

I do know a lot about psychology, and every day I talk to teenagers about the pain in their lives. But it's true, I don't know you.

What I can offer are ideas that work for other people, ideas that are being shown in more and more scientific studies to be effective. And I can try to explain them to you in ways that make sense to young people I work with and may make sense to you as well.

Will these ideas work for you?

I hope so.

But there's only one way to find out, and that's to try them. Try them openly and honestly and if some ideas help then use those ones. If other ideas don't work for you, then read on, and see what else there is. If no ideas help, then keep looking because there are other good ideas out there too. Near the end of this book I'll give some ideas about ways to find further help.

I don't know you.

But I know a few things about you.

I know that sometimes life hurts like hell for you. Maybe a bit of the time, maybe nearly every minute of every day is agony. Sometimes the pain is sadness, sometimes worry or anger or shame or grief or some feeling that you don't even have words for.

Everyone has pain. And I still can't imagine how painful it is for you. Because it is your pain, almost as if it is part of you.

And it hurts.

I know your pain makes sense. If I'd been through what you've been through (and all the other things you've been through before that) then I could feel the way you do too.

Sometimes other people have told you to get rid of your pain.

Your mom may have told you that "You'll be OK" (is she suggesting that you're not OK when you're sad?)…

Your grandfather may have told you that "You've got nothing to worry about. Back in my day…"

Your uncle may have said, "You're just doing it for attention…"

Your teacher may have said that "Now's not the time, just do your work…"

You may not even want your friends to know how much it hurts…

And other people just don't get it…

Of course you're trying to be happy.

And yet it still hurts.

Maybe it even hurts more after they've said those things.

In this book we will talk about the **stuff that sucks**, and the **stuff that makes the stuff that sucks suck more**. We'll notice how trying to fight your pain can make it so much more painful, and how the System—friends, family, school, media, advertising, government, and almost everyone else around you—encourages you to waste so much time in a losing battle.

Then we will look at **stuff that matters** to you— your values—and some ways to figure out what they are and how you can get closer to them. We will also discuss **stuff that is here and now** to help you be more mindful and get some distance from the **stuff that is just stuff**, all those thoughts and feelings which feel big and important but can get in the way of you working toward what really matters to you.

And as I said before, I truly appreciate you being open to these ideas, trying them out, and deciding if they make sense to you.

None of the concepts in this book were developed by me. The ideas come from acceptance and commitment therapy (ACT), which was developed by Steven Hayes and other psychologists. ACT helps people work toward their own set of values, and let go of the unending and exhausting fight against painful thoughts and feelings. The approach makes sense to me, and the tools help me when I use them in my own life and when I work with young people. I found my own ways to explain the ideas and that's what I'm sharing here. If you're keen to know more about ACT after reading this, there are reading recommendations on the final page of this book.

Before we begin...

Notice what it feels like to be breathing in…

Notice what it feels like to be breathing out…

Notice all the thoughts that try to distract you…

Notice any painful feelings that come up and see if you can let them be there, rather than trying to ignore them or push them away…

Notice the thoughts that come up, telling you to try and ignore those feelings or push them away...

Notice the **stuff that sucks**…

WORRY

Some days life can be terrifying. Everyone else seems to know what to do and know what to say, yet it can feel like you don't even know how to be. Huge worrying thoughts come up.

Stuff like:

— What's everyone else thinking about me?
— They're judging me.
— They'll think I'm not confident.
— They'll laugh at me.

And while your brain is saying all that stuff, your body is busy having a freak out:
— Sore stomach
— Hard to breathe
— Heart racing
— Sweaty
— Red face
— Shaky
— Nauseous

And more…

It can feel like everyone is watching and the only reason they aren't commenting is to be polite.

Worry sucks.

SADNESS

Everyone has a different word for their sadness. Some call it a depression or a raincloud, or a fog. It can feel like being smothered by a heavy grey blanket. Everything looks bleak and feels too hard.

It's hard to sleep, but you also feel too tired to get out of bed. You can't concentrate or care about anything. It's too difficult to start new things and finishing anything is out of the question. You might feel like you can't cry even though you want to.

Your mind thinks about all the crap stuff that has happened and the awful stuff that will one day happen, and tells you that you're useless and that you're stupid for thinking like this when so many other people have it so much worse.

Your body becomes heavy and slow. Thoughts even slower. Your mind may go to all sorts of scary places—running away, hurting yourself, even suicide.

Sometimes the grey blanket can start to lift after a few days, although at the time it feels like much longer. Or it might be smothering for weeks or months and the more you try to push it off, the heavier it feels.

Sadness has an important role in our lives. But it can be so hard to think of that when you're alone, stuck under a heavy grey blanket.

heavy grey blanket

LONELINESS

We live in a world that tells us to be an individual and to be independent, yet that doesn't always feel safe. Sometimes being different feels like a painful and lonely place.

It doesn't matter how many friends you have or how close they are. There are days when it feels like no one really gets you. That you're just playing a role, acting like the person you're supposed to be. But deep down you feel totally different. Disconnected even.

And the more you want that connection, the more distant or wrong you feel.

You try to say all the right words and do all the right things and play the right games, and still you feel alone and different. Like no one will ever truly understand how weird and isolated you feel. And you're not sure you'd want people to know anyway. You wonder if others would even stick around if they could see the true you.

You try to be funny enough or smart enough or cool enough so that you can fit in.

Yet it can still feel like you're just filling in time until they find out the truth. Discover that you're a fraud and an imposter. Or discover that you're fundamentally broken and not worth loving.

ANGER

It can be hard to think straight when you're feeling angry. Or to act rationally. Or to want to act rationally.

It seems much more satisfying to yell, swear, smash things, make hurtful comments, threaten violence, or even to be violent.

At least in the short term.

Maybe your anger is masking sadness or worry. That's another thing that sucks. And can lead to shame.

Incredible Hulk

GRRRRRR

Red Mist

Volcano about to blow

SHAME

Of all the emotions in the world, shame can be the hardest to talk about. Often it's even the hardest to think about. The memory of THAT THING you didn't mean to do or mean to say, but somehow happened anyway. That person you never meant to be, but became. The memory gnaws away at you. It probably doesn't even feel like a memory; instead it's like it's happening over and over again—each time you try to do something different but end up doing or saying the same thing again.

You can see it and feel it—in your winded stomach, in your red face, in your tight fists.

Others may even tell you that it wasn't that big a deal, but they don't get it. It was the worst thing.

Ever.

Shame can suck more than anything.

And some
emotions
just feel
like this

And no words seem right to describe them.
Language can't do justice to how awful it feels.

BAD STUFF

As well as all those painful emotions, we also live in a world where really bad stuff can happen.

— Parents fighting or divorcing
— Friends or family getting sick or dying
— Injuries and accidents
— Bullying
— Abuse
— Rape
— Trauma
— Break-ups
— Rejections
— Betrayal

If any of these things have happened to you, then you might be holding on to a pain that's so raw that it hurts to even look at it or touch it.

A pain that burns while everyone else around you seems to be able to get on with their lives.

A pain you didn't ask for but are stuck carrying around.

STUFF MINDS SAY

And while you're trying to deal with those emotions and those experiences, you also have to put up with your mind saying stuff like...

— I suck.

— I'll fail everything.

— No one will ever get me.

— Everyone hates me.

— If anyone found out my secret, my life wouldn't be worth living.

— No one else feels like this.

— I can't trust anyone.

— My parents don't care.

— Everyone is looking at me.

— No one is looking at me.

— No one would care if I died.

— I hate myself.

— I didn't ask to be born.

— I'm fat.

— I'm ugly.

— I'll never live that down.

— I'll be like this forever.

— It's too hard.

— He hates me.

— And so much other **stuff that sucks**…

Yep, sometimes, you feel and think things that suck.

But wait, it gets worse, because the world around you makes stuff suck even more…

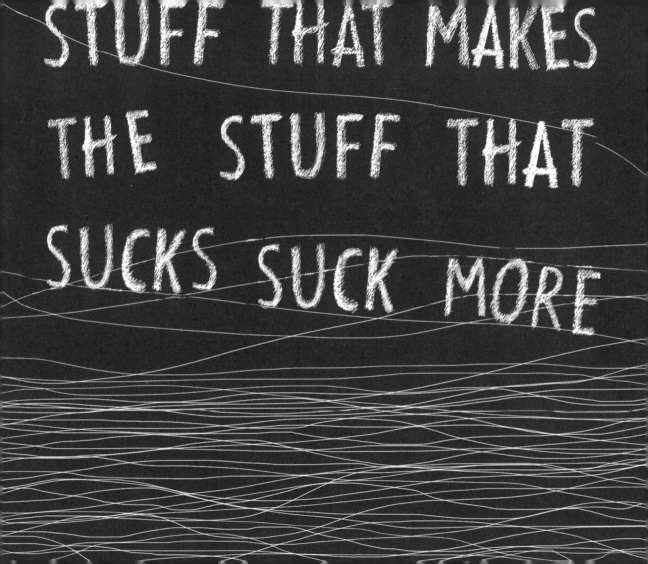

Your mind says stuff that feels mean and those mean things play over and over.

Each of us has thoughts that are painful; each of us struggles with our own recurring themes. We all have minds that say self-critical things and these thoughts can make it much harder to do the things we need to do.

Sometimes it might feel like it would be better if you could just have a lobotomy and get rid of your whole brain.

Except of course, minds are useful. It's actually pretty hard to get anything done without one.

Maybe instead of cutting out your brain, it would be helpful if you thought about how come you have one in the first place? Because minds are fantastic at doing what they're designed for. Unfortunately they weren't designed for the 21st century.

Imagine if the only mobile phone you could have was made ten years ago and you were trying to use up-to-date apps on it. The phone would go really slowly and crash from time to time. Even if it was

state-of-the-art ten years ago when it first came out, it would still struggle with today's environment. But if you threw it out, you wouldn't be able to call anyone at all.

Brains were state-of-the-art technology when they first came out. Back in the days of cave people, our minds were the best brain technology in the world. Compared with the brains of mammoths or saber-toothed tigers or any other creatures, our brains were awesome. They were so good at doing their job that humans could survive and prosper despite those other animals being bigger or faster or stronger than us.

BRAINS

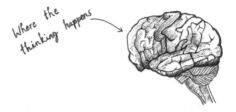

Where the thinking happens

Brains are the ultimate survival tool.

How did brains help us survive? Specifically how do those big, overdeveloped frontal lobes help us survive? The frontal lobes are the part of the brain where the thinking happens. The part we call our "mind." The part that other animals have less of.

So how do minds help us survive? By being on the lookout for dangers!

Every clever thing our minds can do developed to stop us from being eaten by ferocious animals (or being harmed in some other way).

Humans learned to label and form categories so we could say, "I've never seen that particular yellow and black striped animal before, but it looks a lot like other yellow and black striped animals that I call 'tigers' so I better keep away from it."

We learned to make comparisons so we could say, "This path looks safer than that path."

We learned to calculate and problem-solve so we could think of ways to get out of danger or make traps to catch food or handle other survival challenges.

This doesn't mean that Stone Age minds thought about danger all day. When our cave-dwelling great-grandparents were safe at home in their caves, they thought about how to create fire or what shape they should make that wheel they were inventing.

But at the first sign of danger—maybe a nearby growl or twig snap—straightaway Grandpa Og would focus on the threat.

Even today, if you were working on an assignment or chatting to a friend and you heard a loud bang or a crash, straightaway you would stop what you were doing and try to figure out what the noise was and make sure that you and everyone else was OK.

Our minds were designed to be on the lookout for danger and that is still their number-one job. However that can be easy to forget, as there aren't a whole lot of saber-toothed tigers walking down the street trying to eat us anymore.

So when your mind is full of worries, it is not doing anything stupid or harmful. It is doing what it was designed to do, looking out for what could hurt us.

21st CENTURY DANGER

In the 21st century, what is the biggest danger you face? What is the main thing your mind should be on the lookout for?

— Earthquakes?
— Terrorism?
— Global corporations?
— Reality TV shows?

These things can all be pretty damn scary but we know from the aftermath of disasters that people can get through all sorts of horrible situations as long as they have support from others. Having your house fall down would be awful but it would be a million times more awful if you had no one who would let you stay with them or lend you clothes or money or give you a hug or listen when you need to talk.

Maybe the biggest danger we have in these modern times is social rejection (this was a big danger in Stone Age times too, because without other people we would quickly become tiger food). Fitting in with people you want to fit in with is vital for survival. You want friends and family to love you, employers and others to give you a chance, and strangers to help you on the street if you collapse.

Research on social isolation backs me up on this. All sorts of studies show how bad social isolation is for your physical and mental health. We need other people. Some people like having lots of friends, some prefer just one or two close friends, but we all need other people.

So if your mind's number-one job is to look for dangers and the number-one danger in the world is social isolation, then it isn't surprising that your mind looks for signs that you might be rejected.

— Does she like him more than she likes me?
— How will I cope if I'm alone forever?
— Why does no one understand me?
— Etc., etc., etc.

Your mind isn't trying to beat you up. It's looking for dangers so you can stay safe and connected.

And yet it does feel like your mind is beating you up. These thoughts, these worries, can feel horrible. How come?

I blame the system...

HOW THE SYSTEM SETS YOU UP TO FAIL

Chances are your parents and teachers, as well as politicians and celebrities, all encourage you to succeed—they want you to try your hardest and make the most of your life.

On the whole that's a really good thing. Nothing sucks more than people wanting you to fail or setting you up to get it wrong.

But sometimes the System can inadvertently set you up to fail.

The System teaches you that you're supposed to be happy all the time and other feelings aren't OK.

— When you're feeling sad, people say, "Cheer up."
— When you're feeling worried, they say, "Don't worry."
— When you're feeling angry, they say, "Calm down."
— When you're grieving, you're told that, "You'll be fine soon."

On TV everyone is happy, or at least they're happy by the end of forty-three minutes plus ads (and in the ads everyone is happy because they're drinking the right drink or wearing the right shoes).

On Facebook and Tumblr everyone is talking about how great their lives are and how happy they are.

Not surprisingly, we have thoughts that there's something wrong with us if we don't feel happy all the time. To make things worse, people constantly tell us to feel the opposite of what we're actually feeling.

Yet the world is often a terrifying and infuriating place. It makes sense that sometimes we feel sad or worried or angry or whatever.

Can you see how there are some seriously mixed messages coming your way?

STONE AGE MIND MEETS MODERN SOCIETY

Your mind's job is to be on the lookout for danger, which means it is looking for signs that there is something wrong with you, something that could cause social rejection. However, society teaches that you should be happy all the time if you want to be normal. If you're not happy all the time, if you sometimes have other emotions, then you can end up feeling abnormal or broken.

How can you always be happy in a world that is so full of sad and scary and unfair stuff?

Sometimes it can make you just want to scream.

You don't want to feel like there's something wrong with you, so you try hard to not feel sad.

But what happens if you're feeling sad and someone says, "Cheer up"? Do you cheer up? Or do you still feel sad? Maybe you feel even worse. Maybe you're still sad about whatever made you sad, and now you have one more thing to be sad about—that you're sad when you're not supposed to be. You might start thinking that there's something wrong with you.

A huge amount of pain and suffering comes not from your feelings of sadness, worry, anger, or other emotions—instead it comes from trying so hard not to have these emotions. That is the stuff that really sucks.

PURPLE COWS

The world can make thoughts difficult too.

How many times have you been told that you need to think more positively? Or that you can't have any doubt if you want to succeed? That you shouldn't dwell on the negative stuff?

People saying these things might be trying to cheer you up, but these "positive" thoughts can actually be negative. Because when you try to stop thinking about doubts and negative thoughts, you're destined to fail. I'll tell you why.

Remember that your mind is there to protect you from dangers and it does this by thinking about all the current and past and possible dangers it can come up with. This is a really useful strategy if the danger is a tiger or anything external. But what happens if the danger is a thought?

The more dangerous a thought is considered to be, the more you'll think about it. The more you try not to have "negative" thoughts, the more you'll have them. Maybe it's not even fair to call them "negative" thoughts when they're only trying to keep you safe.

Let me demonstrate what I mean about thoughts.

Try thinking about anything you want, but don't think about purple cows…

Keep going for a bit longer.

Remember you're not allowed to have any thoughts
about purple cows…

What happened?

Did you think about purple cows? Or maybe you focused really hard on something else and didn't think about purple cows—and then your mind relaxed and…hello purple cow.

How many times had you thought about purple cows before today? Not often, maybe never at all. But as soon as I said don't think about purple cows, then moo, there's the thought.

And if this happens with purple cows, how much more intensely will it happen with thoughts that you believe are dangerous or scary or painful? Such as those thoughts the System tells you not to have.

Eek, it certainly seems like the System sets us up to be miserable by telling us that we're supposed to be happy and positive all the time. The more we try to avoid negative thoughts, the more we have them and the worse we feel.

LABELS

As well as being told what emotions you should or shouldn't feel, you also get defined by others. You might be known as the Brainy Smurf, who always does well at school, or the Class Clown who is expected to make jokes at all times, or the Wild One, who is always up for doing something crazy.

Sometimes it's fun or convenient to know your role in the group. And I'm guessing that there are other times when you've felt really trapped by everyone else's expectations. They've placed you in a box and it's hard to see a way to be anything else.

Brainy Smurfs can be terrified by every test, because if they do badly then they can feel like they've lost their entire identity. And if they're not brainy, what are they?

Wild Ones can feel like it's not OK to have a quiet night or to not be the drunk and outrageous one. They're terrified of how others would see them if they stepped outside their normal role.

Usually we know that there is more to us than whatever label others have stuck on us. But sometimes it's hard to remember that. Sometimes we hold on tightly to a label that people have given us, for fear of what will be left without it.

What labels have you been given?
Are there labels you have even given yourself?

The Pretty One? Trendy?

The Camp One?

Dumbo?

The Bitch? Introvert?

Emo? Tough Guy?

Freak? Nerd?

Metal-Head?

Skinny?

I bet it was really painful when you felt trapped by expectations.

It was probably even more painful on the days when you believed your own label. When it stopped feeling like a label and started feeling like a fact, it started feeling like You.

Instead of being someone who sometimes does well on tests, you became Brainy Smurf, with all the added pressure that brings. You were quiet at one party and became The Introvert, which made it harder to talk at other parties. You made mean comments and you're The Bitch. One incident that one night and you're The Slut. Soon it's no longer a label, it's You.

And maybe you find that although you hate that it's You, you also feel worried about what might or might not be there if you let go of your label. Your mind might even tell you that there would be nothing left. And that's a terrifying thought.

But wait, it gets worse...

BACK TO THE STONE AGE

Remember our Stone Age friend Og? His mind was busy looking for dangers. When he saw a tiger in the distance, his body got ready to run away or kick some tiger butt or whatever else he learned from watching Discovery Channel's *Saber-Toothed Tiger Special*. So his fear response kicked in—his heart rate went up, his stomach tightened, his muscles tensed, and his focus was purely on the tiger. This was an excellent survival strategy.

Then one day instead of seeing the tiger himself, Og's buddy Gog yelled out "TIGER!" What did Og do? Did he calmly look over to see what Gog was talking about? Not a chance. As soon as Og heard the word "TIGER!" he reacted as if he'd seen the tiger himself—he became tense, worried, and focused on dealing with the threat.

This is one of the ways that humans help each other survive against much bigger or faster foes—good old-fashioned teamwork. We hear a word (or even think a word) and react instantly as if the threat is right there. And it is not only for threats. If you hear the word "cake" you might feel hungry or if you hear the word "puke" you might feel gross. You hear a word or think a thought and your body feels like it's happening right now.

Let's go back to the words that the System has made dangerous in modern times like sadness, failure, rejection, fat. Using the tiger principle described above, you can see how when you think a word, you might feel that it's true and happening right now. If you think "I might fail," you instantly feel like you already are a failure. If you think about a label, it feels true.

So then you try to think less negatively and say to yourself, "Think 'don't fail.'" Except what do you notice about that sentence? Yep, it still contains the word "fail" and triggers emotions associated with failing.

So then you try Positive Thinking, just like so many people have told you to do. You say to yourself over and over, "I will succeed," and it feels sort of great, until sooner or later your mind thinks "I must keep thinking about success because I don't want to think about failing." And BOOM, the fail feelings have sneaked back in.

And maybe the "I will succeed" thoughts didn't feel completely true either, and only triggered more thoughts like "Will I really succeed?" or "What if I don't?" or "What about those times I failed?"

A FULL-TIME JOB

The more you try not to have certain thoughts and certain feelings, the more you'll have them. The more you try to be always happy or confident, the worse you might feel.

Yet you've tried so hard to avoid these thoughts and feelings.

Have a look at this list. Which of these have you used to try to avoid unwanted thoughts and feelings?

Distraction
Positive thinking
Wearing a 'mask'
Drinking
Staying in your room
Pretending everything is OK
Unnecessary spending
Pretending to be sick
Sex
Medication
Pre-emptive strikes against friends
Chocolate

Over-exercising
Drugs
Oversleeping
Facebook
Keeping off Facebook
Skipping class or work
Procrastination
Purging
Thought-stopping
Missing parties
Lying

Acting like you don't care
Cancelling plans at the last minute
Denial
Not returning calls / messages
Making plans to hurt yourself
Shoplifting
Hair pulling
Yelling
Other stuff?
Cutting

If you're anything like me or any other human I've ever met, I'm guessing you've tried a bunch of the things on that list. Maybe you do some of those things every single day.

And how much has it cost you?

Trying to have total control over all thoughts and emotions and keeping some away can be a full-time job.

How often have you missed out on doing things that really matter to you because you're too busy doing what the System tells you, too busy trying to not feel sad, worried, or angry?

For example, you might say, "I won't ask that person out because I'll feel sad if they say no."

Or "I won't study for this exam because every time I think about it I feel worried."

Or "I won't say how I really feel, because I might be rejected."

If you focus on avoiding sadness, worry, anger, guilt, shame (like we all do from time to time) then there's no energy left for the **stuff that matters**—friends, family, creativity, learning, justice, or whatever else you really care about.

And that really sucks...

SO WHAT'S THE ANSWER THEN?

OK, so maybe by now you've noticed that the more you try not to feel sad or worried, the worse you feel. And the more you try not to think certain thoughts, the more you think them. And the more you get stuck fighting these thoughts and feelings, the less time and energy there is for other stuff.

But what's the alternative?

If you can't fight them, maybe you could try not fighting them? Let them be there without struggling against them.

This may sound like a crazy idea. Letting painful stuff be there sounds, well, painful.

Why should you put up with all those painful thoughts and distressing emotions?

What is the point of it all?

C'mon, already,

what is the point?

THE POINT

Remember when you were sitting in Values Class at school, debating the meaning of life and...

Wait, what did you say? Your school never taught values? You were never encouraged to discuss the meaning of life or the Point of it all? You just studied algebra and poetry and rocks and then somehow, by the end of school, you were expected to know what you wanted to do with life and why? Or maybe you went to one of those schools where they told you what your values were supposed to be, whether they felt true to you or not.

These days there are so many options about what you can do and where you can do it. It can be terrifying to make a choice. Paralyzing, even. Sometimes there are so many directions you could go in that it feels safer and easier to try to stay where you are and not move at all.

But of course, that doesn't work. Even if you're not yet sure what your values are, the System doesn't let you stay still. If you don't know what you value, you might just get pushed in the directions that the System values.

As I said at the start, I don't claim to have all the answers—please don't believe anything just because I say it. However, I am keen to share my thoughts about the meaning of life, so if you want to, feel free to keep reading...

Turn the page and you'll see what I think the Point is. Read it, think about it, and see if it is something that makes sense to you too. If it does, then maybe it will be a helpful idea. If it doesn't, no problem, the rest of the book will still make sense, just insert your own views about the meaning of life whenever we talk about values. Or insert the idea that maybe one day you'll have more of a clue about the Point of it all.

Anyway, here's what I think:

Figure out what you care about...

and then care about it.

That's it.

That's what I think the meaning of life is.

I know it can be really hard to know what you care about, so the next section contains some exercises that can help you figure out what stuff really matters to you. After that, we'll look at ways you can focus on the **stuff that is here and now**, so that you can actually do something about the **stuff that matters**.

JUST RIGHT

Have you ever had a time when everything just felt right or meaningful? It may have been a day or an hour or only one second, but for that period of time, none of the sad stuff or scary stuff or stressful stuff mattered, for that moment things just felt true.

I can remember one night when I went to a beach and made a bonfire with friends. We stayed the entire night, telling stories, playing guitar, and having some deep conversations. Eventually we watched the sun rise over the sea.

As I write about it now, it sounds kind of corny and clichéd, but if I let go of those judgments and instead come back to the emotions and sensations, I can remember that at the time the universe just felt right.

Another time I was travelling through New York, and I got a message that my first nephew had been born. I was so excited, I went around the hotel where I was staying telling every stranger I could find, just wanting to share my genuine happiness.

Think of one of those times for you, then once you have read this paragraph, I'd like you to close your eyes and take yourself back to that moment. Notice what it feels like to be there again. Who are you with? What are you doing? What emotions do you feel? Where do you feel it in your body?

OK, begin now. I'll see you on the next page in a minute.

What was that like?

What made that moment so special?

Did the moment you chose feel so right because it connected to something that you really value? You may have been with friends or family or animals or nature or in a creative zone, but I'm guessing that there was a powerful connection for you.

THE VISITOR

Imagine that you're sitting where you are right now doing what you're doing right now (that shouldn't be too hard to imagine), and then the door opens and in walks a person who looks vaguely familiar. You realize that the person looks familiar because it's You in ten years' time. Future You tells Present You that you've come back in a time machine for a really quick chat. I know that imagining even having a future might be difficult, but somehow you've made it. This Future You is compassionate, not a bully, and they're on your side.

Time is short, so Future You jumps straight into telling you stuff that really matters. What do they say?

Listen to Future You for a few minutes and notice how your body feels as they talk to you.

Does Future You give advice? Remind you about things that you really care about, but somehow forget from time to time? Warn you about what will happen if you keep doing what you are doing (but says it in a caring way, not in an "I told you so" lecture).

Were the things Future You reminded you about things that really matter to you? Things you value?

Do you have any questions to ask your future self? How do they answer?

Then it is time for Future You to leave. But first Future You turns back and says one more thing. What is it? What do you notice in your body as Future You says that final thing?

Sit with that feeling for one more minute...

VALUES

"Values" is a word that gets thrown around a lot. We hear about "corporate values" or "family values" or the "value of objects." But it feels like there isn't enough discussion about what values really are.

And when we do talk about values we often end up resorting to big, fluffy words like "respect" or "love" or "trust" or other words that sound great, but can feel so big that they become meaningless or difficult to hold on to.

When I talk about values, I mean the stuff that really matters to you. Once you get past all the critical thoughts and passing emotions, what is left? What was it that made that moment in the past feel so right? What was it that Future You told you with only a brief moment to tell you something?

I spend lots of my time talking to people about their values, and they frequently mention things like friends, family, relationships, learning, trying new things, creativity, animals, the environment, social justice, hobbies, or spirituality.

Do any of these things have meaning for you? There might be other things that you value. I'm not here to tell you what your values are or should be, but I can share an exercise that might help you separate what is important to you from what is absolutely vital.

Why is it important to figure out what is vital to you?

Because values give you a direction to move in.

If you don't know what direction you want to move in, then you keep moving anyway but have no idea if you're getting any closer to where you want to be.

Values are also important because everyone else tries to push their values on you. Parents, friends, school, government and big corporations all want you to move in directions that they value. If you don't know what you value then you'll get pushed in other people's directions. Being pushed all the time can hurt a lot.

DIRECTIONS

Let's take a look at a list of values. Rate each of the items using the scale below. Please actually write the numbers down, because we're going to come back to them.

1 = It doesn't matter much

2 = It's kind of important to me

3 = It's important to me

4 = It's very important to me

5 = It's vital to me

These items don't need to be ranked, they could all be 5s if they all feel equally vital. Values can change—you don't have to commit to these values forever. What matters is that they're meaningful to you now.

Being a good friend _____

Being a good boyfriend / girlfriend _____

Being a good son / daughter _____

Being a good brother / sister _____

Being a good student _____

Being a good employee _____

Being good to myself _____

Being active in my hobbies _____

Being creative _____

Being productive _____

Being a good community member (whatever community means to you) _____

Being a good member of humankind (social justice) _____

Being a good Earthling (the environment, animal rights, or whatever else is important) _____

Being connected to my spirituality (whatever spirituality means to you) _____

Being...(insert another idea here)_____ _____

Being... (insert another idea here)_____ _____

How did you find doing that exercise? When I do it, I find that some values are obvious and clear to me. Others are important to me, but feel further from my reach, so it's harder to rate them as vital. For example, at times in my life when I was single, it was easy to live according to my value of being a good friend, but it was more difficult to live according to my value of being a good boyfriend.

Walking the Walk

Let's go back and look at each value again, thinking about how on track you are for each. Do your actions show that this is something you value? Grab a different color pen and for each value, give it a second rating with this scale:

1 = Totally off track with this value (if you watched me for a week you wouldn't see me do anything that tells you I value this idea)

2 = A bit off track

3 = Mostly on track

4 = On track

5 = There could be a photo of me in the dictionary next to this value

What did you notice when you gave yourself this second rating?

When you rate yourself on doing **stuff that matters** to you, did you say "woohoo" or did you say "crap?" Are you feeling on track or off track? If you're like most people, you probably feel kind of on track with some values, and a bit off track with others.

So how do you go about getting more on track with the stuff that's important to you?

GETTING ON TRACK

Imagine if you met someone sitting at a train station who told everyone how great it is to go West. "West is the way of the future," he says. "We should all keep moving in that direction."

A year later you pass the same station and the same guy is there, in the exact same spot, still telling everyone they should go West. "You need to move West to achieve a meaningful life," he proclaims. "It is the path to happiness and satisfaction."

A year later you pass the same station and the guy is still there. Right there. He hasn't moved one inch in a westerly direction. This time you stop and ask him why he is such a big fan of going West, and he tells you about all the things he has read about the direction West, recommends some useful websites, and even shows you some pictures he has cut out of pamphlets depicting things you will see if you go West. You ask him what is the best thing he has ever seen while travelling West, and he shakes his head.

"I've never been any more West than here, too many bumps along the way. I'm waiting for them to

fix up the track so it will be a smoother journey," he tells you. "But," he adds proudly, "I haven't moved even one inch East in the past few years."

How seriously would you take that man's advice to go West? If West is the way to go, maybe it's worth travelling over some bumps to make progress in that direction.

Values are like compass directions. They're meaningless unless you move.

Saying that you really like going West doesn't mean a whole lot if you don't take at least a small step in that direction. That doesn't mean it's always going to be easy to move West or that you can move miles in that direction every day. Some days it feels like there are things pulling you in every direction or stopping you from moving at all. The blocks might be thoughts, feelings, memories, physiological sensations, or other people and their rules. But it's still worthwhile to move in the directions you care about—even if sometimes you are only able to take tiny steps.

Some days it might feel easy to be the kind of friend that you want to be (assuming that is something you value). You can help a friend with a problem, hang out with them, or give them a hug. Other days it might be hard because you're busy with school or your friends are away or you're feeling depressed or you feel like you don't have any friends at the moment, or whatever... But even on those days, it is possible to take a tiny step toward this value. For example, you could send a brief message or smile at someone that you'd like to become closer friends with or just be at places where you might get to meet people who have the potential to become friends.

Sometimes the direction you value might not be the same direction other people around you are going in. The step you take might not always give you lots of Likes on Facebook. But it will still be a step that you value.

As you take steps, you pass landmarks that tell you that you're moving in the right direction. These landmarks are your goals. Some landmarks take a few steps to get to, others are miles away, but

they are all things that you can pass and that will make you more confident you're on track.

Without a direction, landmarks don't tell you much. Without landmarks, you have no idea if you're making any progress.

Without values, goals aren't meaningful, they're just distractions. Without goals, you don't know if you're living according to the stuff that really matters to you.

For example, if you value traveling, then you might make a goal to learn a hundred words in another language or to save a certain amount of money. Without a valued reason to do these things, they may feel like a chore. Without having specific goals to work toward, how would you know you are getting closer to your trip?

The great thing about valued steps is that it doesn't matter whether they are big steps or small steps, as long as they are in the right direction.

0.01

Imagine there was a reality TV show about your life, and it showed everything that you did in a week. If I watched that show, would I be able to tell what you really value? How about if I read all your status updates and blog posts for a week? Would they reflect the direction you're trying to move in? Could I see what your values are through your small day-to-day behaviors or are you waiting until you can do some grand gesture? How long have you been waiting for that?

Have a look back at the vital and on-track ratings you gave for each value. Which ones did you rate as vital?

If you wanted to raise the on-track ratings for the two or three values that you consider the most vital, what could you do today? How would you raise an on-track rating by 0.1 or 0.01 or 0.000001?

Don't try to raise the score by a whole point or make any dramatic changes. This isn't about setting yourself up to fail or to crash and burn. Remember, it doesn't matter how big the step is as long as it's in the right direction. In fact, small changes are the best changes because they're the ones that are most likely to actually happen. This means they're the things that are most likely to actually make a difference and bring you closer to what you care about.

Write down five things that you could do today that could raise those on-track scores by 0.1 or even 0.01:

1. _____

   _____

2. _____

   _____

3. _____

   _____

4. _____

   _____

5. _____

   _____

What happened when you tried thinking about what steps you'd like to take today? Did your mind tell you that now isn't the time? Did memories from the past or worries about the future make it difficult to choose a task?

That's what happens to me sometimes when I try to think of valued steps I could choose. Which is why we need to be able to bring ourselves back to **stuff that is here and now.**

Remember Og and his Stone Age mind that is focused on looking out for danger? To be ready for danger, he needs to be thinking about what will happen next and what might jump out and kill him. He also needs to be thinking about the past: How does this situation compare with other situations he's been in? What things around him have caused pain in the past?

So our minds love thinking about the future and the past. They're a whole lot less bothered by the present because they're already there. Og doesn't need to prepare for this moment because it's already happening.

Yet Og can't directly change the future and certainly can't change the past. Right here, right now is the only time Og can do anything about anything (although he will hopefully do something that will make his future better too).

In general, things aren't good or bad in the present—they just are. They only become good or bad once your mind judges these events. You might wonder how they will affect you in the future, how you will cope if this continues, or how these things compare with what happened in the past. Of course, there are some things that happen which are obviously bad in the present, say when you injure yourself. But still, your worries about how this injury will affect you in the future, or how it compares to past pain, will increase the suffering.

These judgemental thoughts about past and future can be very upsetting and even physically painful. So you try really hard to keep those thoughts out of your head. You might have tried distraction, chocolate, alcohol, drugs, the Internet, or even self-harming. You may have avoided places that could trigger memories or put off important conversations that might cause distress. Did any of these strategies help? Did you find that you got a break from the sensations or thoughts in the short term, but long term things still felt the same? Maybe these avoidance strategies even made you feel worse in the long term.

You might find that trying to keep control over all your thoughts and feelings is an exhausting game, a game you can't win and wish you hadn't played. Remember what I said about purple cows—the more you focus on not thinking about something, the more you think about it.

The more you try to not feel sad, the sadder you feel.

What would happen if instead of trying to avoid all that stuff, you let it be there? Watched it with curiosity? Stayed in the present even while your mind tries to drag you away into thoughts about the past and future? Would you be freer to live in the now?

If you put less energy into trying to control things that are virtually impossible to fully control (like the stuff you think and feel), you'll have more energy to focus on things that you can control. The stuff you do. The stuff that matters.

Bringing your awareness back to the **stuff that is here and now** is a really important way to live a more valued life that you have control over. It will allow you to let go of the fight against those mean thoughts and free up energy to make your life more like the life you want. This can help you prevent always being pushed by others in the directions they want. It will be useful, whether you've already got some ideas about what your values are or if you're still in the process of figuring them out.

You don't need to be in the now all the time, but also you don't want to never be here.

It's not easy to be in the here and now. Anytime you try to focus on the present, your mind will do all it can to bring judgements back in. These judgements can make focusing on the present not just difficult, but even dangerous. For example, judgements like "This will affect me badly," "Others will laugh at me and not get it," or "I tried something similar in the past and it didn't work."

In the next section we'll talk about how to take our minds less seriously, but for now let's try being in the here and now.

THE MOMENT

Ever had a hug that just felt right, so meaningful that you were totally in the moment? Maybe it even allowed those thoughts about your past or future to feel less overwhelming for a brief time.

Have you ever been so into a conversation with a friend that while you were listening nothing else mattered?

Or climbed a tree and looked, really looked, at the view?

Your senses help you engage with the **stuff that is here and now** and it's a powerful way of taking a step back from the dark or critical places that your mind can take you to.

How do you know where you are right now?
— Have a look around; what can you see?
— Listen; what can you hear?
— Breathe in; what can you smell?
— Lick your lips; what can you taste?
— Reach your hands out; what can you touch?
— What does it feel like in your body?
— What temperature is it?

COME TO YOUR SENSES

Your senses tell you where you are, they provide your mind with the information it needs so it can do its job of judging and comparing and calculating and more judging.

If they made a reality TV show about your life, your senses would be the raw unedited footage, before your mind comes in to do all the editing required to create stories.

Here are a whole bunch of activities that put one or more senses to work. This is your chance to watch some unedited footage of yourself that your senses have collected, without the critical reality TV director leaping in to edit.

Please don't just read the ideas, actually go and try a few of them and notice what it feels like to be in the present. Notice how many ways your mind tries to convince you not to do these activities or tells you afterward that it didn't count or that you weren't doing it right.

FEEL THE MUSIC

Put on a song. Not too loud, but loud enough that you can give the song your attention. It could be a song you particularly love or it could be a song that just happens to be on the radio (this will work better if there's no music video accompanying it).

Can you be inside the song?
— What is each instrument doing?
— What do the instruments do together?
— How fast is the song?
— Where in your body do you feel it?
— Can you feel it in your feet?
— In your shoulders?
— Deep in your heart?

How about the words?
— Can you hear the emotion?
— Can you be truly present with the
   singer's emotions?

If possible, try not to make the song about you, but instead listen to the singer's joy or sadness and notice what it feels like to connect with them. What emotions come up for you while you're listening?

Notice what it feels like to be having the emotion.

What images are conjured up?

Observe them as if they are on a TV screen in front of you.

feel the moment

TASTE THE CHOCOLATE

SEE THE SEA

Get a box of chocolates that contains many different flavors of chocolate. Pick one without looking.

Roll it around your fingers. What shape is it? What texture is it? How heavy is it?

Smell it. What can you notice? Where in your body do you notice it? Does it trigger sensations in your mouth or your stomach? Notice your breath as you take in its aroma.

Gently place it in your mouth. What is the first thing you taste? Is it sweet? Fruity? Bitter? What does your tongue feel like when it makes contact with the chocolate?

Put it in your mouth. Roll it around your mouth. What tastes and textures do you notice? Take a bite. Observe the flavours. What happens in your body while you eat it?

And when your mind tries to distract you with judgements or critical thoughts, notice this, then again turn your attention back to the tastes and smells and textures.

Sit down in a place where you can see a body of water. It might be the ocean or a river or a pond.

And look. Really look. Spend two or three minutes observing all you can see in the water. Is there movement? Or stillness? What color is it?

What other senses can you use to experience this water? What does it sound like? What does the air around you smell like? Can you taste it? What does it feel like to be sitting in that place?

What thoughts, emotions, and memories arise? Notice how they try to distract you. Can you acknowledge them and then bring your attention back to the water?

Or try one of these ideas:

— Hug a friend.

— Walk up a hill and look at the view. How many different shades of green can you see?

— Clap your hands in different rooms and notice how the sound is different in each room.

— Hold an ice cube and feel it melt.

— Stand in a sunny spot and notice where on your body you can feel the heat.

— Eat a wasabi pea and notice what happens in your mouth and nose each second.

— Rub moisturzser onto your hands slowly, observing the feeling in each part of your hands.

— Drink a cup of tea, coffee, or hot chocolate, noticing the smell, steam patterns, temperature and of course, the taste.

— Dive into a swimming pool and note the change in temperature.

— Eat a whole meal without talking, watching TV, checking your phone, reading or anything else— just focus on the smells and textures and taste of what you're eating.

— Wrap your arms around yourself and give yourself a hug.

— Hold a rock; observe its texture, temperature, weight, and color.

— Belly laugh for one minute, even if nothing is funny.

— Put your pencil to a piece of paper and draw something without any planning or goals.

— Wash your hair, notice what it feels like as the water and the shampoo touch each part of your head.

— Play with a cat or dog.

And here is some room to write down other activities that involve senses that you've done in the past or would like to try.

_____

_____

_____

_____

_____

What happened when you tried these things? Did you find that the **stuff that sucks** didn't stop sucking, but when you were focusing on your senses it didn't seem to matter so much?

Did you feel connected to something other than your suffering, even if only for a brief moment? Those mean thoughts and painful emotions still suck, but even with that stuff could you feel a connection with the here and now?

PORTABLE ANCHORS

Connecting to your senses can help you feel more grounded and possibly even stronger or more ready to deal with stuff around you. The problem is that you don't always have a wasabi pea or a shower or a friend to hug immediately at hand. And you're not always by the sea or able to crank up the music.

Wouldn't it be great if there was something that you had with you all the time that you could use to help feel connected to **stuff that is here and now**?

Portable anchors can help you connect to the present wherever you are. Here are two I like:

The orb

Imagine a small floating orb of light. Watch it sit in the big toe of your right foot. What does it feel like right now in your right foot? Do your best not to judge it (even if your mind still hands you judgemental thoughts), instead just notice it.

Then feel the orb move to the next toe and notice what that feels like.

Slowly let the orb move around each part of your foot, then the other foot, then up each leg, through your stomach, chest, shoulders, down each arm and into each hand, back up through your neck and face, all the way to the top of your head. Pause in each spot and just observe what it feels like there. Don't try to change it or judge it. Just notice the **stuff that is here and now.**

Breathe

Your breath is an anchor. It's always there, yet most of the time you don't notice it. So when you do focus on it, it becomes a sensory experience that can bring you back to the here and now.

Chances are that at some point in your life, someone has suggested that you do some kind of breathing exercise when you're feeling worried or angry.

"Just take a deep breath."

"Breathe in for five and out for five."

"Do square breathing."

"Stomach breathe."

"Imagine you are blowing up a balloon."

Or one of the other million breathing exercises out there.

Almost all breathing techniques are helpful, although lots of them may be too long or complicated to remember at a time when you're feeling stressed or angry or panicky or overwhelmed. Your mind might even try convince you that breathing won't work or is silly. But if you already have one technique that works for you then keep doing it when you need it.

Or try this one:

Notice what it feels like to be breathing.

That's it—don't try to control your breath or change it. Just observe it. Notice what it feels like to be breathing in. Notice what it feels like to be breathing out. Notice the breath in your stomach, lungs, throat, mouth, nose, or wherever it is. You can't be more here and now than when you're breathing.

That is all there is to that exercise. Set your phone to beep in two minutes' time and spend those minutes just noticing your breath.

And don't wait until you're having a bad day before you try this exercise. Try it each day for two minutes so that at times when you feel you're really struggling to find your breath, you've already practised this skill. Otherwise you'd be like a pianist who waited until you were performing in front of hundreds of people before you looked at the music you had to play. The performance would go better if you had already practiced the piece in a quiet, calm place.

STUFF THAT IS HERE AND NOW AND INSIDE US

Our senses help us become more aware of what is happening in the world around us.

Our breath and the imagined orb help us be aware of what is happening in our body.

And as we do those things we can also notice that there is other stuff happening right here, right now.

We think. We feel.

I think, therefore I think.

Have you ever noticed what it feels like to be thinking? Even the question sounds a bit strange. Normally we're so busy thinking that we don't notice that we're thinking. We don't realize that all the noise in our heads is just thoughts.

For the next two minutes, please put down this book and notice what it feels like to be thinking. Even notice what it feels like to be thinking about thinking. As thoughts come up, notice that you're having a thought. When judgements come up, notice that you're making a judgement.

See you in two minutes.

What was that noticing like?

Did your mind give you reasons to stop noticing thoughts and to get back to actively thinking? To being in the middle of your thoughts rather than watching them? My mind frequently does that when I try this exercise. Minds love to think, that's their job. So it's not surprising that your mind tries really hard to get you to stay deep in the middle of your thoughts, rather than to step back and notice that you're doing the thinking. It wants you to stay in the middle of the reality TV show, rather than notice all the editing, CGI, and sound effects that have been added to the raw footage to create a compelling story.

Hearts just want to pump blood, livers want to remove toxins, spleens want to do whatever spleens do, and minds want to think. And as we've noticed before, that can be an incredibly useful tool for survival, and also thinking can be helpful with school, work, and everything else you might want to do.

Yet sometimes it is helpful to step outside your mind and notice that you're thinking. To notice that the stories you're being told by your mind are not the full story, and that trying to figure out the "full story" may just be one more game your mind plays to keep you thinking.

If we actually took in all the information all our senses gave us all the time, we'd hit information overload really quickly. So our minds can help the process by creating categories and short cuts and labels and stereotypes to help us get as much information as quickly as possible without overwhelming us.

As we noticed earlier, sometimes the stories and labels that our minds create may sound so believable or be so familiar that we try to hold on to them even if they're not working for us. Sometimes we give the stuff more attention than it deserves.

At the start of this book I suggested that you **don't believe a word I say.** At least, don't believe it because I say it. Believe it if you've tried it and it feels helpful.

I'm now going to push my luck and suggest another thing:

Don't believe a word *you* say (or think)—or at least, don't believe it because you think it. Believe it if you've tried it and it feels helpful.

Remember your mind evolved to protect you from danger and pain. And some thoughts feel so painful that they become dangerous and your natural inclination is to try to avoid them. But remember, the more dangerous you think a thought is, the more you will have that thought.

So you might say, "I can't take this exam because it will show people that I'm stupid."

Or "I can't ask that person out because they might think I'm ugly."

And once that belief is there, then you need to find a way of getting rid of it before you can move forward with your life. In the meantime you put off studying or asking that person out.

Sometimes it doesn't even feel like a belie;, it feels really true. Or you really hope that it isn't true, but you still worry that it is.

You argue with the thought and try to convince yourself it isn't true. And what happens? Did you notice that the more you argue with the thought, the more it argues back? Sometimes your good thoughts win, sometimes the mean thoughts win. Either way, you lose because all the time you spent arguing is time you weren't able to get anything done.

Just like we saw with purple cows, **trying to get rid of thoughts doesn't get rid of them, it just wastes energy.** Trying to win an argument with your mind doesn't take you any closer to the life you want to live. It just makes you feel tired. If you're always fighting the **stuff that is just stuff** then there's no time to be.

LIVING WITH ANNOYING FRIENDS

Have you ever had a friend who you enjoy hanging out with, but sometimes they say really dumb things or stuff that you really disagree with? You've possibly had times when they said something annoying and you rolled your eyes or smiled at someone else nearby and then kept doing whatever it was you were doing. Other times maybe you got angry at them for what they said and tried to tell them why they were wrong. Or maybe you ruined the rest of your day by leaving or even refusing to go out because they were going to be there. It's true that they said the thing that was wrong or annoying, but the bit that ruined your day was you trying to make them less wrong or less annoying.

If we multiply that by a million, you get your mind. Your mind can be your best friend, coming up with all sorts of interesting and creative ideas or making you laugh. It can also help you manage your day-to-day life, school, job, relationships, and so on.

Then sometimes (or most of the time in a bad week or month) your mind will say mean stuff or dumb stuff or stuff that really hurts. And you get the choice of whether you try to fight it or get angry with it and end up ruining your day. Or instead you could roll your metaphorical eyes and keep hanging out with your mind anyway. The thoughts are still there, but they haven't ruined your day.

MAKING FRIENDS WITH YOUR MIND

How about giving those thoughts a name? Or imagining what your mind would look like if it was that friend who is sometimes annoying? So when it starts up with some of those same old messages (which are probably starting to get boring anyway), listen to what they say. Then return to what you are intending to do—being a good friend, a good partner, a good family member, a good athlete, a good human, or whatever it is that you value doing at this moment.

The stuff that your mind says to you may hurt or generate some painful emotions. But, like a friend, it may sometimes say some hurtful things while coming from a well-meaning place (to keep you safe and to help you avoid social rejection). You might find you don't want to put as much energy into the losing battle of trying to argue with your mind to get rid of those mean thoughts.

I'm sure that right now your mind is throwing lots of buts at you, trying to convince you that what it says aren't just thoughts that can be shrugged off. It's telling you that what it says is true and important and life will go badly if you don't listen.

BUT MY THOUGHT IS 'TRUE'.

Is it?

Is it even possible to be true?

I don't know what your specific thought is, but maybe it is something like:
— I'm stupid.
— I'm ugly.
— I'm unlovable.
— I suck.

Are those thoughts true or false? We already saw that the more you argue with a thought the more it argues back, and that is easy for your mind to do because those thoughts are neither true nor false.

The statement "I'm stupid" looks like a full sentence so you might treat it like one. But actually by itself it doesn't mean a whole lot.

Compared to Einstein, you may well be stupid; compared to a piece of chalk, you're probably quite intelligent. Compared to some friends, you might struggle in some areas, but you're also smarter than them in other areas. By itself the statement "I'm stupid" is neither true nor false, which is why you can't win an argument with your mind against that thought. And as soon as you try to win the argument, you've already lost, because your mind keeps getting to do all the thinking it wants to do and in the meantime you've made no progress on stuff that you genuinely care about.

Other arguments you can't win because they're about things that are in the future. For example, your mind might say, "The party will go badly" or "I'll always be like this." It doesn't matter how much you argue with these thoughts, you can't win because they're about things that haven't happened yet.

BUT IT DOESN'T FEEL LIKE A THOUGHT.

Yep, minds are sneaky. They can hide thoughts in all sorts of ways—in other people's voices or as a really vague sense of doom or as an absolute fact.

But unless you're hearing voices, chances are that those ideas are coming from your thoughts, even if they are hiding in disguise. And even if you are hearing voices, it may be that they connect to thoughts you're having too.

Maybe if I just told my mind to shut up more loudly or in a different way, it would actually shut up.

Possibly. If you could find a way to turn off your brain then you would be free of those mean thoughts. You could do this with distraction, sleeping, drugs, hurting yourself, or those other things we talked about on page 36. And you might get a short break from those comments. Unfortunately you will also not be able to get anything you value done or go anywhere. If you want to take steps toward stuff you actually care about, if you want to fight for human rights or connect to your spirituality or be successful in your career, then you will need to bring your mind along—even though some pretty harsh thoughts will come along for the ride.

THE BIG STUFF

Emotions can cause so much pain. Sometimes you might wish that you could turn off your emotions. Or some of them at least.

So why do you have to have emotions? Is there a need for them or are they just poor design?

Emotions are your body's way of letting you know that you care. Sadness, worry, anger—these all tell us that we care about others, care about ourselves, or care about the world.

It can really hurt when someone you love doesn't love you back. Or when life doesn't go the way you'd planned. Or when really bad, horrible stuff happens to you or to someone you love. **And at the same time, wouldn't it be so much worse if you didn't feel sad about these things?** Wouldn't that mean that you didn't care in the first place? Or that you'd given up hope that things might go well sometimes?

Worry comes up when you're doing something and you value the result. Without worry about exams or first dates you wouldn't bother preparing and trying to get it right. Sometimes your mind tries to distract you by creating worries about other things, perhaps things that don't matter to you so much. Chances are that behind those worries there are deeper worries that your mind is trying to keep you away from. Stuff that really matters to you.

Anger is how you feel when you see injustice. Maybe you've been mistreated or maybe someone or something you care about is mistreated. Maybe you feel it in your fists or your voice or your feet. Maybe you see red. **Without anger you wouldn't stand up for justice.**

And without being able to feel every other emotion, how could you possibly relate and genuinely connect with others? Because everyone else is feeling these emotions too.

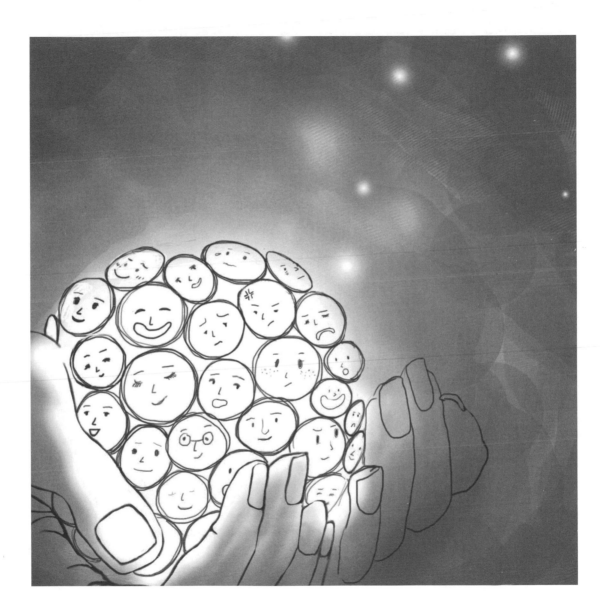

BUT WHY DOES IT HAVE TO HURT SO DAMN MUCH?

Why does it feel like the sadness will go on forever?

There are two parts to an emotion:

HOW YOU FEEL

and

HOW YOU FEEL ABOUT HOW YOU FEEL

Emotions come in and go out and while they are inside they can hurt, but they always pass.

Unless you try to fight them.

If you say you can't have this emotion because it will stick around too long or it will hurt too much or ruin your life or others will think you're weak or…

Yep, there are a million and one things your mind tells you about your emotions that will make you think that you shouldn't have them. It will tell you that they need to be fought. Obviously, the System encourages this by telling you how long your emotion is supposed to last or how intense it is allowed to be. For example, friends might tell you to "just get over it" (whatever "it" is). Your favorite TV character gets over a relationship break-up by the end of an episode. Film characters may even get a montage to help speed up the process: a song plays while we see lots of scenes to show us weeks or months have passed until they feel better again.

In real life, sadness and grief take as long as they take.

What happens when you try not being sad? Do you still feel sad? Plus now you have one more thing to be sad about—that there's something wrong with you for feeling this sad. The more you try to not have an emotion, the more you have it.

SO WHAT'S THE ALTERNATIVE?

Let the emotion be there.

Where is the emotion sitting in your body right now? Is it in your stomach? Your chest? Your heart? Your eyes? Your fists?

Wherever it is sitting, see if you're able to notice it. Observe it with curiosity and caring. Like you've just landed inside this body and you're experiencing this emotion for the first time. See if you're able to sit with it for a minute or two without trying to push it away or tell yourself that it's not supposed to be in there. And when the thought comes up telling you that you need to push the emotion away, see if you're able to observe that thought with curiosity and caring too.

And remember three things:

1. Every emotion will pass (provided you don't fight it).

2. Emotions mean you care.

3. No one else (including your own mind) has the right to tell you how you should feel or how bad you should feel it or how long you should feel it.

THIS IS NOT A TRICK.

The first few times I read about the idea of making space for emotions and allowing them to be there, I got excited. I thought that if I could just find a way to be truly willing and ready to have the painful emotions and to allow the mean thoughts and labels to be there, then I wouldn't have to have them anymore. Like it was some kind of cunning reverse-psychology trick where I could just say that I don't mind being sad and the sadness would go away.

It took me much longer to understand that this isn't how it works. Being willing to feel my pain isn't another strategy I can use to avoid my pain. It is genuinely accepting that sometimes stuff really sucks. Sometimes life can really hurt. Sometimes this world isn't what I signed up for. Sometimes I still feel like I would do anything not to have these feelings and these thoughts.

Maybe I'm just a slow learner. Especially when it comes to the really painful stuff.

You might find it comes a lot quicker than it did for me. Probably the acceptance comes and goes. Willingness to allow suffering to be there is hard. Damn hard. And often frightening too.

And the only thing harder is not being willing to allow suffering to be there.

PUTTING IT ALL TOGETHER

Stuff sucks.

The world can be a nasty place that can trigger all sorts of unwanted thoughts and feelings.

The System sucks.

People around you, no matter how well-meaning, can make you feel like the thoughts and emotions you're having are not OK, that you're crazy or mentally ill or just plain wrong. These messages are strongly reinforced by advertising, social media, Hollywood, and pretty much everywhere else you look.

Trying not to have particular thoughts and emotions is hard work.

And it doesn't work. The more you struggle against these internal experiences, the more you will have them. And even when you know it doesn't work, you'll still keep struggling against them because that's what millions of years of evolution combined with our culture have taught us to do.

Trying not to have these thoughts and emotions takes lots of energy.

Which means there isn't much energy left to put into doing **stuff that matters**—perhaps being the kind of friend you want to be, or the kind of family member you want to be, or the kind of human you want to be. And not being able to take steps toward **stuff that matters** creates more of the **stuff that sucks**—the sadness, the guilt, the worry, the self-criticism, and so on.

SMALL STUFF HELPS

Take small steps toward stuff that you value. Getting just a little bit closer to living the life that you want to live makes putting up with the **stuff that sucks** worthwhile (but won't stop that stuff from being painful).

In order to do the small stuff you've got to know where you are, even when your mind is worrying about what might happen in the future or what has happened in the past. Bringing your attention back to the **stuff that is here and now** can help you feel more aware of where you are and what you need to do to get closer to the **stuff that matters** to you. Your breath and your senses are helpful when you need to bring yourself back to the **stuff that is here and now**.

Thoughts will keep on coming. That's their job. They're going to do all they can to identify dangers and then keep you away from them. Dangers might be man-eating tigers, or they might be social rejection or negative judgement by others. And

when your mind thinks of these scenarios, you will feel the emotion as strongly as if the scenario or thought is really happening right now.

Allowing thoughts to be there, holding them lightly without trying to argue with them or ignore them or push them away, can be hard work. Sitting with your emotions, even the ones you really wish that you didn't have or didn't have as intensely, can be incredibly hard. But it's worth doing if it frees up your energy to focus on the **stuff that matters** to you.

Please don't believe any of these ideas just because I say so. But if you do try the ideas, and they help you live a life that is closer to the life that you value, then that is exciting.

And if you've tried them all, and you still need more support, here's some **other stuff that helps**.

Other Stuff That Helps

Self-care

Have you noticed that it often feels easier or more socially acceptable to look after others than it does to look after yourself? Often we know what advice to give others but forget to give the same advice to ourselves.

What would happen if you treated yourself like someone you care about? Would you take better care of yourself? Even if your mind tells you that you don't deserve self-care, maybe you're actually still someone you value? And even if you struggle to value yourself, did you know that looking after yourself increases the chance that others around you will look after themselves, even if you don't tell them directly what they should do (which usually doesn't help anyway)?

There are a range of things that you can do that have been shown to increase your energy and improve your mood and confidence (but of course they won't fully get rid of unwanted thoughts or emotions).

The most basic place to start is with eating and sleeping. Your body will feel better if you eat more fruit and vegetables, and will feel worse if you eat too much junk food. Yet despite that, it is really common for your mind to try to encourage you to eat crap food when you're feeling down. So to take care of yourself, you'll need to notice those thoughts, take a few breaths, and then eat something healthy anyway.

Similarly with sleep, your mind can give you a hundred reasons to stay up late. It might tell you that there are fun things to do, or that you'll miss important discussions online, or that if you're lying in bed without something to distract you then your mind will go to places you really don't want it to. But giving yourself the chance to have enough hours to sleep is one of the most important things you can do for your health. It recharges all your cells to give your next day the best chance possible to go well. If falling asleep is difficult, then make sure you turn off all screens (laptop, tablet, TV, smartphone) at least half an hour before you plan to go to sleep and instead do something calming, such as reading a book or having a cup of hot chocolate. Then once in bed in the dark, that is a good time to practice the breathing exercises we discussed. Notice what it feels like to breathe in. Notice what it feels like to breathe out. And when your mind

tries to distract you, acknowledge the thought, then bring your attention back to your breath.

Regular exercise is one of the most important things you can do for your physical and mental health. It can help with your confidence, your mood, your focus, your worries, your sleep…the list goes on. Stretching or yoga are particularly helpful because they also allow you to focus on the **stuff that is here and now.**

Reducing the amount of bad stuff you put into yourself is also an effective way to make yourself feel better. Stopping or cutting down on alcohol, cigarettes, and other drugs will make it easier for you to take steps toward the **stuff that matters** and help you feel like your life is more on track. And remember small improvements are likely to be the most effective—don't try to change everything at once.

As I said at the very beginning of this book, don't do these things just because I told you to. Try them and **if they work for you** and allow you to live a more valued life **then keep doing them.**

Seeing friends face-to-face

One of the first things that can happen when you begin to feel sad or worried or isolated or any other big emotion is that you might reduce contact with friends. It can be really common for your mind to try to overwhelm you with thoughts like:

— They won't get it.
— They'll think I'm just attention-seeking.
— They've got their own problems to deal with.
— They wouldn't like me if they found out what I'm really like.
— Hanging out with people feels like too much work at the moment.
— I won't enjoy it.
— They should have called me by now.

And so on.

Maybe your mind has said some of these things to you, or maybe it has come up with its own sneaky ways of getting you to reduce social contact so that you have more time alone, thinking and worrying.

Yet it's also likely that when you rated values, friends were rated as very important or vital. Friendships are worth cultivating and maintaining even when you're struggling. Especially when you're struggling.

Friends can help you feel connected to the world and to the stuff that matters to you. They can give you some space from all that **stuff that sucks**. Even though the pain might still be there, friends can make it easier to breathe, to live.

Friends can also provide smiles, hugs, or ears that listen. Although for any of that to happen, you need to see your friends face-to-face. Online social networks have their uses, but when you're feeling isolated they can increase that feeling as you look at everyone else's online masks and don't get to actually be with people.

Have you ever noticed that when you're feeling sad or worried, sometimes you feel like talking about what is going on, sometimes you feel like talking about anything else, and sometimes you don't feel like talking at all? Those are really common experiences. Equally common is the frustration you might feel when a friend picks the wrong way to try to support you—they try to get you to talk when you don't feel like talking, or try to distract you when you do actually feel like talking. Sometimes when they get it wrong, you might feel even more distant from your friends.

What would happen if you actually ask your friends for what you need, rather than just hoping they know? Maybe say to a friend:

"I don't feel quite ready to talk about it, can we just hang out and talk about it another time?"

Or

"I know you've got your stuff going on too, but is it OK if we talk a bit about some of the stuff I'm feeling worried about?"

Or something along those lines.

Would you want your friend to be able to ask you for what she or he needs? If you're able to ask them for what you need in a gentle manner, that will increase the chance that they will be able to talk to you when they need to.

What if they don't quite get it, or don't say the right thing? Then maybe you can talk to them about that. Or maybe you've got another friend who is better at saying the right thing when you need to talk about stuff, whereas this friend is better at helping you take your mind off your thoughts when you need that.

Please don't ask friends to hold on to secrets that aren't fair to ask them to hold. For example, if you've done something risky or plan to do something risky, friends will need to tell someone.

Parents, teachers and other adults

Sometimes the **stuff that sucks** feels so daunting that trying to deal with it alone or with the help of friends may not be enough.

I don't know your parents, but chances are that they love you to bits and really want to help you, even if sometimes their words or actions don't feel very helpful.

Sometimes parents are better problem-solvers than listeners, and launch straight into telling you what you did wrong or how you should fix it. Even though what may be needed is for them to just listen to how you're feeling. For them to allow you space to have your own thoughts and emotions so you can figure out what you need to do. Sometimes you won't need to do anything except sit with the sadness or the worry, and it can feel helpful to have a parent get that this is what you need and allow you some space. You might even want to show them the parts from this book that talk about letting emotions be there without struggling against them. Or you might want to be quite clear about whether you need them to help you solve a problem or if you need them to listen.

The System your parents grew up with was different from the System you're in now. Mental health and distress were talked about in different ways, and treated in different ways. They may have grown up in a world where young people had more chance of getting a job or the System told them not to feel what they were feeling or think what they were thinking.

So sometimes when you talk to them they may not get it straight away. But please keep trying, because I'm sure that they've picked up that something is wrong and will be keen to help. And they'll be more likely to help in useful ways if you actually let them know what's going on.

And if your parents don't get it or aren't very good at listening then find another adult you can talk to, because the world can suck even more without adults who can help. Aunties, uncles, grandparents, teachers, school counselors, sports coaches, parents of friends…keep looking and keep trying because **you deserve to be supported by someone.**

Professionals

Often when you're struggling, people might suggest that you talk to your family doctor or GP. You might also be taken to see a counselor or psychologist or a mental health service.

GPs are commonly the first professional you'll see when life is difficult. GPs have the advantage that they can think broadly about all the physical and psychological factors that could be making life stressful. They also may know some of your history so have more understanding about why the stress you've dealt with could be causing some of the **stuff that sucks** right now. Unfortunately, GPs usually don't have much time to see you, appointments may only be 10 to 15 minutes long, and that probably isn't enough time to talk openly and to feel genuinely heard. Doctors may suggest medication, and this can help reduce some of the emotional pain and increase your energy to focus on the stuff that really matters to you. But make sure you're given the opportunity to ask any questions you might have about the pills and about the side-effects, and remember there are other options besides medication.

These could include counselors, psychologists, therapists, social workers, family therapists, psychiatrists…

There are lots of different mental health professionals, and they all have different training and different understandings about what causes distress and what will be helpful. If you like the ideas that are suggested in this book and want more support along these lines, then you should ask for someone with training in acceptance and commitment therapy (ACT).

The main thing is that whoever you see and whatever their training or job title is, **you should feel like you're being fully listened to**, and seen as a human, not as a problem that needs to be fixed. The person you're seeing may know a lot about mental health, but you know a lot about you, and it's only when you and the professional combine knowledge that you can find a way to help get your life back on track.

If the person you are supposed to talk to doesn't feel like someone you can talk to, then please ask to see someone else. Life is too short to have professionals judge you or make you feel like you're a problem.

Thank You

I really appreciate you taking the time to listen to these ideas and to try the suggestions out. Remember, small steps can lead to big changes in your life.

These are ideas I really believe in, and the research that shows these ideas really work is strong and gaining more support each year.

This book presents acceptance and commitment therapy using the words I use when I'm working with young people. The concepts of ACT and many of the metaphors come from other contextual behavioural science researchers and ACT therapists.

If you want to read more about Acceptance and Commitment Therapy, I suggest you have a look at these books:

— *The Happiness Trap: How to Stop Struggling and Start Living* by Russ Harris
— *Things Might Go Terribly Horribly Wrong: A Guide to Life Liberated from Anxiety* by Kelly Wilson and Troy DuFrene
— *Get Out Of Your Mind And Into Your Life for Teens: A Guide to Living an Extraordinary Life* by Joseph Ciarrochi, Louise Hayes, and Ann Bailey

I have been very fortunate to attend workshops, conference presentations, and to read books by the following inspirational teachers: Sonja Batten, Joseph Ciarrochi, Russ Harris, Steven Hayes, Kelly Koerner, Jason Luoma, Louise McHugh, Emily Sandoz, Niklas Torneke, Jennifer Villatte, Matthieu Villatte, Robyn Walser, Darrah Westrup, and Kelly Wilson. There are also other people who have contributed to my knowledge of ACT via research articles or chapters, blog posts, conference presentations, and conversations. I am particularly grateful for all the support from my ACT Interest Group in Wellington.

More importantly, I am in awe of all clients and families I have worked with. I have learned so much from you and I am so grateful for all your wisdom, trust, and willingness.

Ben Sedley is a clinical psychologist and acceptance and commitment therapy (ACT) practitioner with over fifteen years of experience working with adolescents and families facing mental health difficulties. Sedley's research and practice has focused on examining children and young people's understanding of mental health, which has helped guide him on the best ways to explain mental health concepts and ACT to young people.

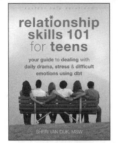

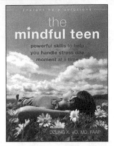

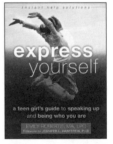